HESI A2 STUDY GUIDE 2023-2024

In Easy-To-Read Format

2023

A DANIEL MELEHI BOOK

©2023

0

Contents

INTRODUCTION

About the Hesi A2

About the Hesi A2

The Hesi A2, or Health Education Systems Incorporated Admission Assessment, is a standardized test used by nursing schools and allied health programs to evaluate student readiness for entry into their programs. The test assesses students' knowledge and skills in several areas, including math, reading comprehension, grammar, vocabulary, anatomy and physiology, and critical thinking.

The Hesi A2 is a computer-based test that consists of 160 multiple-choice questions and takes approximately four hours to complete. The test is timed, and students are allowed to take breaks between sections. The questions are randomized, and each student receives a unique set of questions.

The Hesi A2 is used by nursing schools and allied health programs as part of their admission process. The test helps to ensure that students have the necessary knowledge and skills to succeed in their chosen programs. It is important to note that each school or program may have different score requirements for admission, and students should check with their schools to determine what scores are required.

Preparing for the Hesi A2 is essential for success on the test. There are many resources available to help students prepare, including study guides, practice tests, and online resources. Students should review the content areas covered on the test, practice answering questions, and identify areas where they may need additional help.

In addition to preparing for the content areas, students should also practice test-taking strategies. Strategies such as time management, process of elimination, and educated guessing can help students maximize their scores on the test.

Overall, the Hesi A2 is an important part of the admission process for nursing schools and allied health programs. Students who prepare adequately and use effective test-taking strategies are more likely to achieve the scores needed for admission into their desired programs.

Importance of passing the Hesi A2

One of the most important steps in pursuing a career in healthcare is passing the Hesi A2 exam. The Hesi A2 is a comprehensive exam that assesses a student's academic readiness for nursing school. It is an essential tool used by nursing schools to evaluate applicants and determine their eligibility for admission.

Passing the Hesi A2 exam is crucial for several reasons. Firstly, it is a mandatory requirement for admission into most nursing schools. Without a passing score, you cannot gain admission into nursing school. Secondly, it is an indicator of academic readiness. The exam assesses a student's knowledge of key subject areas such as math, science, English, and anatomy and physiology. Passing the exam shows that you have a solid foundation in these areas, which is essential for success in nursing school.

In addition to being a requirement for admission, passing the Hesi A2 exam can also have a significant impact on your future career prospects. Many healthcare employers require candidates to pass the Hesi A2 exam before they can be considered for employment. Therefore, passing the exam not only increases your chances of getting into nursing school but also opens up more job opportunities in the healthcare industry.

Another reason why passing the Hesi A2 exam is important is that it prepares you for the rigor of nursing school. Nursing school is known for its challenging curriculum, and the Hesi A2 exam is a good indicator of the types of questions and concepts that you will encounter in nursing school. By passing the exam, you have a better understanding of what to expect and can better prepare yourself for the demands of nursing school.

In conclusion, passing the Hesi A2 exam is essential for anyone who wants to pursue a career in healthcare. It is a requirement for admission into nursing school, an indicator of academic readiness, and a significant factor in determining your future career prospects. Therefore, it is important to take the exam seriously and prepare adequately to ensure success.

Purpose of the book

The purpose of this book is to provide an ultimate study guide for all topics of the Hesi A2 exam, specifically for the 2023-2024 testing cycle. The Hesi A2 exam is used by nursing schools as part of their admissions process, and it is crucial for prospective nursing students to achieve a high score in order to secure a spot in their desired program.

This book is designed to help students prepare for the Hesi A2 exam by providing comprehensive coverage of all the topics that are tested on the exam. It includes detailed explanations of the various subject areas, including math, reading comprehension, vocabulary, grammar, anatomy and physiology, and chemistry. Each section is broken down into easy-to-understand chapters, with practice questions and detailed explanations to help reinforce key concepts.

In addition to providing comprehensive coverage of the exam content, this book also includes valuable tips and strategies for test-taking success. This includes advice on how to manage your time effectively during the test, how to approach different types of questions, and how to stay focused and calm under pressure.

Whether you are taking the Hesi A2 for the first time or are looking to improve your score, this book is an invaluable resource for anyone who wants to ace the exam. With its comprehensive coverage of all the topics tested on the Hesi A2, as well as its practical advice and strategies for success, this book is the ultimate study guide for anyone looking to achieve their nursing school dreams. So why wait? Start studying today and get ready to ace the Hesi A2!

UNDERSTANDING THE HESI A2 EXAM

Overview of the exam

The Hesi A2 exam is a standardized test designed to evaluate the knowledge and skills of prospective students in various healthcare fields. This comprehensive test covers a range of topics, including math, vocabulary, grammar, biology, chemistry, and anatomy and physiology. The Hesi A2 exam is commonly used by nursing schools, and other healthcare programs to determine candidates' eligibility for admission.

The exam consists of 8 sections, each focusing on a specific area of study. The sections are as follows: Math, Reading Comprehension, Vocabulary, Grammar, Anatomy and Physiology, Biology, Chemistry, and Learning Style. The exam is computer-based, and each section is timed separately.

The Math section covers basic arithmetic, algebra, and geometry. It tests the candidate's ability to solve mathematical problems using formulas and calculations. The Reading Comprehension section evaluates the candidate's ability to read and understand written passages, while the Vocabulary and Grammar sections assess their knowledge of English language conventions.

The Anatomy and Physiology section covers the structure and function of the human body, while the Biology section evaluates the candidate's knowledge of general biological concepts. The Chemistry section includes questions on basic chemical concepts, while the Learning Style section assesses the candidate's preferred learning method.

The Hesi A2 exam is a crucial step in the admission process for healthcare programs. A high score on the exam can increase a candidate's chances of being accepted into their desired program. Therefore, it is essential to prepare adequately for the exam by studying the relevant content and practicing sample questions.

In conclusion, the Hesi A2 exam is a comprehensive test that evaluates the knowledge and skills of prospective healthcare students. It covers a range of topics and consists of 8 sections, each timed separately. Adequate preparation is necessary to achieve a high score on the exam and increase one's chances of admission to their desired program.

Content and format of the exam

The Hesi A2 exam is a comprehensive test that assesses prospective nursing students' knowledge and abilities in various subject areas. To pass the exam, students need to understand the content and format of the test. This subchapter will provide an overview of what to expect on the exam day, the types of questions, and the format of the exam.

The Hesi A2 exam consists of 8 sections, including math, reading comprehension, vocabulary, grammar, biology, chemistry, anatomy and physiology, and critical thinking. The exam is computerized and can vary in length and time. The exam is not timed, and students can take their time to complete the exam. However, most schools require students to complete the exam within a specific time frame.

The exam consists of multiple-choice questions, fill-in-the-blank questions, and critical thinking questions. The multiple-choice questions have four possible answers, and the student must select the correct one. Fill-in-the-blank questions require students to provide a specific answer. Critical thinking questions assess a student's ability to think logically and critically.

The format of the exam is as follows: students will first complete the learning profile section, which assesses their learning style. Then, they will move to the eight subject areas mentioned earlier. Each section has a different number of questions, and the questions are randomized. Students will not know which section they are on or how many questions they have left.

It is essential to study the content of the exam thoroughly. The Hesi A2 exam is designed to test the knowledge students have gained in high school and college. The math section, for example, covers topics such as fractions, decimals, and algebra. The biology section covers topics such as cells, tissues, and organs. The anatomy and physiology section covers the structure and function of the human body.

In conclusion, the Hesi A2 exam is a comprehensive test that assesses a student's knowledge and abilities in various subject areas. To pass the exam, students must understand the content and format of the test. This subchapter has provided an overview of what to expect on the exam day, the types of questions, and the format of the exam. It is essential to study the content of the exam thoroughly and to practice critical thinking skills to ace the Hesi A2.

Scoring system

The Hesi A2 exam is a comprehensive test that evaluates a student's aptitude in various fields such as math, science, reading comprehension, and vocabulary. Scoring well in the Hesi A2 exam is crucial for students who want to pursue a career in the healthcare field. The scoring system of the Hesi A2 exam is designed to assess the student's knowledge and skills in specific areas.

The Hesi A2 exam consists of several sections, and each section has its own scoring system. The math section of the exam is graded on a scale of 0-100, and a student must score at least 70% to pass the section. The reading comprehension section is also graded on a scale of 0-100, and a student must score at least 75% to pass the section. The vocabulary and grammar section is graded on a scale of 0-100, and a student must score at least 75% to pass the section.

The science section of the Hesi A2 exam is graded on a scale of 0-100, and a student must score at least 70% to pass the section. The anatomy and physiology section is also graded on a scale of 0-100, and a student must score at least 70% to pass the section.

It is important to note that the Hesi A2 exam is a computer-adaptive test, meaning that the difficulty level of each question is based on the student's performance on the previous question. The scoring system takes into account the number of correct answers, the difficulty level of the questions, and the time taken to complete each section.

To score well in the Hesi A2 exam, it is important to have a comprehensive study plan that covers all the sections of the exam. This can include taking practice tests, reviewing study materials, and seeking help from tutors or study groups.

In conclusion, the scoring system of the Hesi A2 exam is designed to evaluate the student's knowledge and skills in specific areas. A student's performance in each section is graded on a scale of 0-100, and a minimum score is required to pass each section. By preparing thoroughly and following a comprehensive study plan, students can score well in the Hesi A2 exam and achieve their career goals in the healthcare field.

STUDY STRATEGIES FOR THE HESI A2 EXAM

Time management techniques

Time management is a crucial skill that every student needs to master in order to succeed in their academic pursuits. The Hesi A2 exam is no exception, and managing your time effectively is essential to ensuring that you cover all the necessary topics and sections on the exam.

Here are some time management techniques that you can use to maximize your study time and increase your chances of success on the Hesi A2:

1. Create a study schedule: One of the most effective ways to manage your time is to create a study schedule. This will help you to stay organized and ensure that you cover all the necessary topics before the exam. Make sure to allot sufficient time to each section of the exam and focus on your weaknesses.

2. Prioritize your tasks: Another important time management technique is to prioritize your tasks. Identify the most important and urgent tasks, and focus on those first. This will ensure that you make the most of your study time and do not waste time on less important tasks.

3. Use time-blocking: Time-blocking is a technique that involves breaking your study time into specific blocks or chunks of time. For example, you could study for 45 minutes, take a 15-minute break, and then repeat the cycle. This technique helps you to stay focused and avoid distractions.

4. Avoid procrastination: Procrastination is one of the biggest obstacles to effective time management. To avoid procrastination, set realistic goals and deadlines for yourself. Break large tasks into smaller, more manageable ones, and reward yourself for completing each task.

5. Eliminate distractions: Distractions can take up a lot of your study time and prevent you from focusing on your tasks. To eliminate distractions, turn off your phone, close unnecessary tabs on your computer, and find a quiet study space.

In conclusion, time management is a critical skill that every student must master to succeed on the Hesi A2 exam. By creating a study schedule, prioritizing your tasks, using time-blocking, avoiding procrastination, and eliminating distractions, you can maximize your study time and increase your chances of success on the exam.

Study materials

When it comes to preparing for the Hesi A2 exam, having study materials that are comprehensive, organized, and effective is key. Fortunately, there are a wide variety of resources available to help you get ready for this important test.

One of the best places to start is with official Hesi A2 study materials. The Hesi website offers a range of resources, including practice exams, study guides, and other helpful materials. These resources are specifically designed to help you prepare for the types of questions you'll encounter on the exam, so they're a great place to start your study journey.

Another excellent resource is a reputable Hesi A2 study guide. These guides are typically written by experts in the field and offer a comprehensive overview of the exam, as well as strategies for approaching each section. Look for a guide that is up-to-date with the latest test format and includes practice questions and detailed explanations.

Online study materials are also a great option for many students. There are a number of websites that offer Hesi A2 practice tests, flashcards, and other helpful resources. These materials can be accessed from anywhere with an internet connection and can be a convenient way to fit studying into your busy schedule.

In addition to these resources, don't forget about traditional study materials like textbooks and notes. Reviewing key concepts and taking notes on important topics can be an effective way to reinforce your understanding of the material.

Ultimately, the key to success on the Hesi A2 exam is to find the study materials that work best for you. Whether you prefer online resources, study guides, or traditional materials, focus on finding materials that are comprehensive, organized, and tailored to your learning style. With the right study materials and a dedicated study plan, you can ace the Hesi A2 and achieve your nursing career goals.

Test-taking strategies

Test-taking Strategies

Preparing for the Hesi A2 exam can be a daunting task, but with the right test-taking strategies, you can increase your chances of success. Here are some tips to help you ace the Hesi A2:

1. Develop a Study Plan

Before you begin studying, create a study plan that outlines what topics you need to review and when you will review them. This will help you stay organized and motivated throughout your studies.

2. Practice with Sample Questions

One of the best ways to prepare for the Hesi A2 is by practicing with sample questions. This will help you become familiar with the format of the exam and the types of questions you can expect to see on test day.

3. Time Management

Time management is crucial when taking the Hesi A2. You will have a limited amount of time to complete each section of the exam, so it is essential to budget your time wisely. Use your study plan to help you practice pacing yourself during practice tests.

4. Read the Instructions Carefully

Before beginning each section of the Hesi A2, make sure to read the instructions carefully. This will ensure that you understand what is expected of you and can answer the questions correctly.

5. Eliminate Wrong Answers

If you are unsure of an answer, try to eliminate any obviously wrong answers. This will increase your chances of guessing correctly and can help you avoid losing points on the exam.

6. Stay Calm

Finally, it is essential to stay calm on test day. If you feel yourself getting anxious or stressed, take a deep breath and focus on the task at hand. Remember, you have prepared for this exam, and you can do it!

By following these test-taking strategies, you can increase your chances of success on the Hesi A2 exam. Remember to stay focused, stay motivated, and stay calm, and you will be well on your way to achieving your goals.

Practice tests

Practice tests are an essential part of any successful Hesi A2 study plan. Not only do they help you identify areas where you need improvement, but they also give you a chance to familiarize yourself with the test format and build your confidence.

When it comes to practice tests, there are a few different options available. First, you can use the official Hesi A2 practice tests, which are available for purchase on the Elsevier website. These tests are designed to mimic the actual exam and provide you with a comprehensive assessment of your skills and knowledge.

Another option is to use third-party practice tests, which can be found online or in Hesi A2 study guides. While these tests may not be as closely aligned with the actual exam as the official tests, they can still be a valuable tool for practice and review.

Regardless of which practice tests you choose to use, it's important to approach them strategically. Here are some tips for getting the most out of your practice tests:

1. Take the test in a quiet, distraction-free environment. Treat it as if it were the actual exam.

2. Time yourself to get a sense of how long you have for each section.

3. Review your results carefully, paying special attention to areas where you struggled.

4. Use your results to guide your study plan going forward. Focus on improving your weaker areas while also reinforcing your strengths.

5. Take multiple practice tests to get a better sense of your progress over time.

Remember, practice tests are just one part of a successful Hesi A2 study plan. Be sure to also review content areas, use flashcards and other study aids, and seek out additional resources as needed. With dedicated effort and a strategic approach, you can ace the Hesi A2 and achieve your academic and professional goals.

ENGLISH LANGUAGE AND GRAMMAR

Parts of speech

As you prepare for the Hesi A2 exam, it's important to have a solid understanding of the different parts of speech. These are the building blocks of language, and being able to identify and use them correctly is essential for clear communication.

Nouns are words that identify people, places, things, or ideas. They can be concrete or abstract, and can be singular or plural. Common examples include "dog," "house," "love," and "idea."

Verbs are words that express action, occurrence, or existence. They can be transitive (taking an object) or intransitive (not taking an object). Examples of verbs include "run," "eat," "exist," and "think."

Adjectives are words that modify or describe nouns. They can be used to indicate size, color, shape, or other qualities. Examples of adjectives include "big," "red," "round," and "beautiful."

Adverbs are words that modify or describe verbs, adjectives, or other adverbs. They can be used to indicate time, manner, place, or degree. Examples of adverbs include "quickly," "happily," "here," and "very."

Pronouns are words that replace nouns in a sentence. They can be used to avoid repetition or to indicate ownership or relationship. Examples of pronouns include "he," "she," "they," and "my."

Prepositions are words that show the relationship between nouns or pronouns and other words in a sentence. They can indicate location, time, direction, or manner.

Examples of prepositions include "in," "on," "at," and "with."

Conjunctions are words that connect words, phrases, or clauses in a sentence. They can be used to indicate addition, contrast, or relationship. Examples of conjunctions include "and," "but," "or," and "because."

Interjections are words or phrases used to express emotion or feeling. They are often used in spoken language, and can indicate surprise, excitement, or frustration. Examples of interjections include "wow," "oops," "ah," and "ugh."

By understanding the different parts of speech and how they work together, you can improve your writing and communication skills. As you prepare for the Hesi A2 exam, make sure to review these concepts and practice identifying and using them correctly in sentences.

Sentence structure

Sentence structure is an essential component of the Hesi A2 exam, and it is crucial to understand the different elements that make up a sentence. The Hesi A2 exam assesses your ability to construct accurate and effective sentences, so mastering this skill can significantly improve your overall score.

Sentences consist of a subject, a verb, and an object. The subject is the person, place, or thing that performs the action, while the verb is the action or state of being. The object is the person, place, or thing that receives the action. For example, in the sentence "Mary ate an apple," Mary is the subject, ate is the verb, and an apple is the object.

There are different types of sentences, including simple, compound, and complex sentences. Simple sentences consist of one independent clause, while compound sentences are made up of two or more independent clauses joined by a conjunction. Complex sentences, on the other hand, contain one independent clause and one or more dependent clauses.

It is also essential to understand sentence fragments and run-on sentences. Sentence fragments are incomplete sentences that lack a subject, a verb, or both. Run-on sentences occur when two or more independent clauses are joined without proper punctuation or conjunctions.

To construct effective sentences, it is crucial to use proper grammar, punctuation, and syntax. Proper grammar includes using the correct tense, subject-verb agreement, and pronoun reference. Punctuation involves using commas, periods, semicolons, and other punctuation marks correctly. Syntax refers to the order of words in a sentence and can affect the meaning and clarity of a sentence.

In conclusion, understanding sentence structure is critical for success on the Hesi A2 exam. It is essential to master the different types of sentences, avoid sentence fragments and run-on sentences, and use proper grammar, punctuation, and syntax to construct accurate and effective sentences. By practicing these skills, you can significantly improve your score on the Hesi A2 exam.

Punctuation and capitalization

Punctuation and capitalization are essential components of the English language that help readers understand the meaning of written words. In the Hesi A2 exam, having a strong grasp of punctuation and capitalization is crucial as it can affect your overall score. This subchapter will provide you with a comprehensive guide on the rules of punctuation and capitalization that you need to know for the Hesi A2 exam.

Punctuation refers to the marks used in writing to separate sentences and clarify meaning. The most common punctuation marks in English are the period, comma, semicolon, colon, exclamation mark, and question mark. Proper use of these marks will ensure that your writing is clear, concise, and easy to read.

One of the most common punctuation errors is the misuse of commas. Commas are used to separate items in a list, separate clauses in a sentence, and to set off introductory phrases or clauses. It is important to note that commas should not be used to separate subjects from verbs or to join two independent clauses without a coordinating conjunction.

Capitalization refers to the use of uppercase letters at the beginning of a sentence or for proper nouns. Proper nouns include the names of people, places, and things, such as New York City, John Smith, or the Statue of Liberty. In addition, the first letter of the first word in a quotation should be capitalized if it is a complete sentence.

It is important to note that consistency is key when it comes to punctuation and capitalization. Make sure to use the same style throughout your writing and avoid mixing different styles. Consistency will ensure that your writing is clear and easy to understand.

In conclusion, mastering the rules of punctuation and capitalization is crucial for success on the Hesi A2 exam. Make sure to practice using these rules in your writing and seek feedback from peers or tutors. With dedication and practice, you can ace the punctuation and capitalization section of the Hesi A2 exam.

<u>Vocabulary</u>

Vocabulary is an essential component of the Hesi A2 exam. It is important to have a strong understanding of the vocabulary used in the exam to be able to comprehend the questions and answer them accurately. In this subchapter, we will discuss the vocabulary section of the Hesi A2 exam, the types of words that are tested, and some strategies that can help you prepare for this section.

The vocabulary section of the Hesi A2 exam consists of approximately 50 multiple-choice questions. These questions are designed to test your knowledge of the meanings of words and your ability to use them in context. The words tested in this section are commonly used in healthcare settings, and many of them may be unfamiliar to you if you do not have a background in healthcare.

Some of the types of words that are tested in the vocabulary section of the Hesi A2 exam include medical terms, prefixes, suffixes, and common English words that have a specific meaning in the healthcare field. For example, you may be asked to identify the meaning of words such as "antibiotic," "hypertension," "dyspnea," or "diabetes." You may also be asked to identify the meaning of prefixes and suffixes such as "hypo-," "hyper-," "itis," or "ectomy."

To prepare for the vocabulary section of the Hesi A2 exam, it is important to build your vocabulary by learning and memorizing medical terms, prefixes, and suffixes. Flashcards are an effective tool for memorizing vocabulary. You can also use online resources such as Quizlet to practice and learn new words.

Another strategy that can help you prepare for the vocabulary section of the Hesi A2 exam is to read healthcare-related articles and literature. This can help you become familiar with the vocabulary used in the healthcare field and improve your ability to understand and use medical terms in context.

In conclusion, the vocabulary section of the Hesi A2 exam is an important part of the exam that tests your understanding of medical terms, prefixes, suffixes, and common English words used in healthcare settings. By building your vocabulary and practicing using medical terms in context, you can improve your chances of performing well on this section of the exam.

MATHEMATICS

Basic arithmetic

Basic arithmetic is a fundamental aspect of the Hesi A2 test. This section of the exam evaluates the test-taker's ability to perform basic mathematical operations, such as addition, subtraction, multiplication, and division. This subchapter will provide a comprehensive overview of the basic arithmetic concepts that you need to know to ace the Hesi A2 exam.

Addition is the process of combining two or more numbers to get a sum. To perform addition, you need to align the numbers vertically, with the ones digit on the right side. You then add the ones digit, carry over any remaining digits to the next column, and repeat the process until you have added all the digits.

Subtraction is the process of taking away one number from another to get a difference. To perform subtraction, you need to align the numbers vertically, with the ones digit on the right side. You then subtract the ones digit from the ones digit, borrow if needed, and continue the process until you have subtracted all the digits.

Multiplication is the process of finding the product of two or more numbers. To perform multiplication, you need to align the numbers vertically, with the ones digit on the right side. You then multiply the ones digit of the second number with the first number, and continue the process until you have multiplied all the digits. You then add up the results to get the final product.

Division is the process of finding the quotient of two numbers. To perform division, you need to align the numbers vertically, with the divisor on the left side and the dividend on the right side. You then divide the divisor into the first digit of the dividend, write down the quotient, multiply the quotient by the divisor, and subtract the result from the first digit of the dividend. You then bring down the next digit of the dividend and repeat the process until you have divided all the digits.

In conclusion, mastering basic arithmetic is essential for succeeding in the Hesi A2 exam. By understanding the fundamental concepts of addition, subtraction, multiplication, and division, you will be well-equipped to tackle any arithmetic question that comes your way. With practice and determination, you can ace the Hesi A2 and achieve your academic and professional goals.

Algebra

Algebra is a fundamental topic covered in the Hesi A2 exam, which tests your knowledge of basic arithmetic, algebraic operations, equations, and inequalities. It is essential to have a solid foundation in algebra if you want to succeed in the Hesi A2 and pursue a career in healthcare.

In this subchapter, we will explore some of the key concepts and strategies for mastering algebra. We will cover topics such as solving equations, factoring, graphing, and word problems. We will also provide you with plenty of practice exercises and tips for improving your algebraic skills.

One of the most important skills you will need in algebra is the ability to solve equations. An equation is a mathematical statement that asserts the equality of two expressions. To solve an equation, you must determine the value of the variable that makes the equation true. There are different methods for solving equations, including substitution, elimination, and graphing. You should learn and practice all these methods to be prepared for the Hesi A2 exam.

Another important skill in algebra is factoring. Factoring involves finding the factors of a polynomial, which is a mathematical expression that contains two or more terms. Factoring can be useful in simplifying expressions, solving equations, and graphing functions. You should learn the different techniques for factoring polynomials, such as factoring by grouping, factoring trinomials, and using the difference of squares formula.

Graphing is also a crucial skill in algebra, as it allows you to visualize the relationship between two variables. You should be familiar with basic graphing concepts, such as coordinates, lines, slopes, and intercepts. You should also be able to interpret and analyze graphs, including identifying the domain, range, and intercepts of a function.

Finally, algebraic word problems are a common type of question in the Hesi A2 exam. These problems require you to use algebraic equations to solve real-life scenarios. You should be able to translate word problems into algebraic equations, solve the equations, and interpret the results in the context of the problem.

In conclusion, algebra is a crucial topic in the Hesi A2 exam, and mastering its concepts and skills is essential for success. By practicing and applying the strategies we have discussed in this subchapter, you can improve your algebraic abilities and achieve your goals in healthcare.

Geometry

Geometry is an important aspect of the HESI A2 exam, and it is essential to understand the basic concepts and formulas to score well on this section. Geometry is the branch of mathematics that deals with the study of shapes, sizes, and positions of objects in space. It is used extensively in different fields, including architecture, engineering, and physics.

The HESI A2 Geometry section tests your knowledge of geometric shapes, angles, lines, and measurements. It is essential to understand the different types of shapes and their properties, such as triangles, circles, rectangles, and squares. You should also know how to calculate the area, perimeter, and volume of these shapes.

Another critical aspect of Geometry that you should understand for the HESI A2 exam is angles. You should know how to measure and classify angles, such as acute, obtuse, and right angles. You should also have an understanding of geometric lines, such as parallel, perpendicular, and intersecting lines.

To prepare for the Geometry section of the HESI A2 exam, you should review the basic concepts and formulas regularly. You can also practice with sample questions and quizzes to test your knowledge and identify areas that need improvement. It is also helpful to understand how Geometry is applied in different fields, such as construction and engineering.

In conclusion, Geometry is an essential subject to master for the HESI A2 exam. By understanding the basic concepts and formulas of geometric shapes, angles, lines, and measurements, you can score well on this section of the exam. Practice regularly and review the material to ensure that you are adequately prepared for the HESI A2 Geometry section.

Trigonometry

Trigonometry is a branch of mathematics that deals with the study of the relationships between the sides and angles of triangles. It is an important topic in the Hesi A2 exam as it is used in various fields such as engineering, physics, and astronomy. In this subchapter, we will cover the basics of trigonometry, including the definitions of sine, cosine, and tangent, and how to use them to solve problems.

Firstly, let's define the three main trigonometric functions: sine, cosine, and tangent. Sine is defined as the ratio of the opposite side to the hypotenuse of a right-angled triangle. Cosine is defined as the ratio of the adjacent side to the hypotenuse of a right-angled triangle. Tangent is defined as the ratio of the opposite side to the adjacent side of a right-angled triangle.

To solve trigonometric problems, we use the properties of these functions. For example, if we know two sides of a right-angled triangle, we can use the Pythagorean theorem to find the third side. We can also use the trigonometric functions to find angles. For example, if we know the length of two sides of a right-angled triangle, we can use the inverse trigonometric functions to find the angle opposite the known sides.

There are also special angles that are commonly used in trigonometry. These are $0°$, $30°$, $45°$, $60°$, and $90°$. By knowing the ratios of the sides of these special angles, we can easily solve trigonometric problems involving them.

In conclusion, trigonometry is an important topic in the Hesi A2 exam and is used in various fields. By understanding the definitions of sine, cosine, and tangent, and how to use them to solve problems, you can improve your score in the Hesi A2 exam. Additionally, by memorizing the ratios of the sides of the special angles, you can solve trigonometric problems more efficiently.

ANATOMY AND PHYSIOLOGY

Introduction to human anatomy and physiology

Introduction to Human Anatomy and Physiology

Human anatomy and physiology are two closely related fields of study that are essential to healthcare professionals. They help us understand the structure and functions of the human body, and how they work together to maintain life. If you're planning to pursue a career in healthcare, knowledge of human anatomy and physiology is crucial. This subchapter will provide you with an introduction to the study of human anatomy and physiology and its importance in the healthcare industry.

Human Anatomy

Anatomy is the study of the structure of the human body. It involves the identification and classification of organs, tissues, cells, and the various systems that make up the body. There are two types of anatomy: gross anatomy and microscopic anatomy. Gross anatomy deals with the study of structures that can be seen with the naked eye. Microscopic anatomy, on the other hand, deals with the study of structures that are too small to be seen with the naked eye.

Human Physiology

Physiology is the study of how the body functions. It involves the study of the various systems of the body, including the respiratory system, cardiovascular system, and nervous system, among others. Physiology also deals with the study of how these systems work together to maintain life.

Importance of Human Anatomy and Physiology

Human anatomy and physiology are important in the healthcare industry for several reasons. First, healthcare professionals need to understand the structure and function of the human body to diagnose and treat diseases and injuries. Second, knowledge of human anatomy and physiology is essential for medical research, drug development, and clinical trials. Third, understanding human anatomy and physiology is important for public health, as it helps us understand how diseases spread and how to prevent them.

Conclusion

In conclusion, human anatomy and physiology are two closely related fields of study that are essential for healthcare professionals. They help us understand the structure and functions of the human body, and how they work together to maintain life. By having a basic understanding of human anatomy and physiology, you'll be better prepared to pursue a career in healthcare and make a positive impact in the lives of others.

The skeletal system

The skeletal system is a critical component of the human body, providing support and protection for our internal organs, as well as allowing us to move and perform various tasks. It is made up of bones, cartilage, and ligaments, and is responsible for a variety of functions, including maintaining the shape of the body, producing blood cells, and storing minerals like calcium and phosphorus.

The human skeleton consists of 206 bones, each with its own unique shape and function. Some of the most important bones in the body include the skull, which protects the brain; the ribs, which protect the heart and lungs; and the spine, which allows us to stand upright and supports the weight of the head and upper body.

In addition to bones, the skeletal system also includes cartilage, which provides cushioning between bones and allows for smooth movement, and ligaments, which connect bones to one another and provide stability to joints.

Maintaining a healthy skeletal system is crucial for overall health and well-being. Regular exercise, especially weight-bearing activities like walking and running, can help strengthen bones and prevent conditions like osteoporosis, which can lead to fractures and other complications.

Other factors that can impact skeletal health include diet and lifestyle choices. Consuming adequate amounts of calcium and vitamin D, for example, can help keep bones strong and healthy, while smoking and excessive alcohol consumption can weaken bones and increase the risk of fractures.

In summary, the skeletal system plays a vital role in the human body and is essential for maintaining overall health and mobility. Understanding its structure and function is key to passing the Hesi A2 and pursuing a career in healthcare.

The muscular system

The muscular system is one of the most important systems in the human body. It is responsible for movement, stability, and posture. Without it, we would not be able to walk, run, or even stand upright. In this subchapter, we will discuss the structure and function of the muscular system, including its various types of muscles.

The muscular system is made up of three types of muscles: skeletal, smooth, and cardiac. Skeletal muscles are attached to bones and are responsible for voluntary movements such as walking and lifting weights. Smooth muscles are found in the digestive system, blood vessels, and other internal organs. They are responsible for involuntary movements, such as the contraction of the stomach during digestion. Cardiac muscles are found only in the heart and are responsible for its rhythmic contractions.

Muscles are made up of bundles of muscle fibers, which in turn are made up of myofibrils. Myofibrils are composed of two types of protein filaments called actin and myosin. When these filaments slide past each other, the muscle contracts. This process is called the sliding filament theory and is the basis for all muscle movement.

Muscles also require a constant supply of energy to function. This energy comes from the breakdown of adenosine triphosphate (ATP) molecules. ATP is produced through a process called cellular respiration, which occurs in the mitochondria of muscle cells.

In addition to movement, the muscular system also plays a key role in maintaining posture and stability. Muscles work in pairs, with one muscle contracting while the other relaxes. This allows us to maintain balance and stability while standing or sitting.

To summarize, the muscular system is an essential part of the human body. It allows us to move, maintain posture, and perform a variety of other functions. Understanding its structure and function is an important part of preparing for the Hesi A2 exam.

The nervous system

The nervous system is a complex network of cells, tissues, and organs that work together to control and coordinate the functions of the body. It is responsible for receiving and processing sensory information, controlling muscle movements, and regulating the body's internal environment.

The nervous system is divided into two main parts: the central nervous system and the peripheral nervous system. The central nervous system includes the brain and the spinal cord, while the peripheral nervous system includes all of the nerves that extend from the brain and spinal cord to the rest of the body.

The brain is the control center of the nervous system and is responsible for processing and interpreting information from the senses, controlling muscle movements, and regulating the body's internal environment. It is also responsible for higher cognitive functions, such as thinking, memory, and emotion.

The spinal cord is a long, thin, cylindrical bundle of nerve fibers that extends from the brainstem to the lower back. It serves as a conduit for information between the brain and the rest of the body, and is responsible for reflexes, such as the knee-jerk reflex.

The peripheral nervous system is divided into two main parts: the somatic nervous system and the autonomic nervous system. The somatic nervous system controls voluntary movements, such as walking and talking, while the autonomic nervous system controls involuntary functions, such as heart rate, breathing, and digestion.

The autonomic nervous system is further divided into two branches: the sympathetic nervous system and the parasympathetic nervous system. The sympathetic nervous system is responsible for the body's "fight or flight" response, which prepares the body to respond to a perceived threat. The parasympathetic nervous system is responsible for the body's "rest and digest" response, which promotes relaxation and digestion.

In conclusion, the nervous system is a complex and intricate network of cells, tissues, and organs that work together to control and coordinate the functions of the body. Understanding the structure and function of the nervous system is crucial for success in the healthcare field, and is essential knowledge for anyone preparing to take the Hesi A2 exam.

The circulatory system

The circulatory system is one of the most important systems in the human body. It is responsible for transporting blood, oxygen, and nutrients throughout the body, as well as removing waste products and carbon dioxide.

The circulatory system is made up of three main parts: the heart, blood vessels, and blood. The heart is a muscular organ that pumps blood throughout the body. It is located in the chest, between the lungs, and is about the size of a closed fist. The heart has four chambers: the right atrium, the right ventricle, the left atrium, and the left ventricle.

Blood vessels are the tubes that carry blood throughout the body. There are three types of blood vessels: arteries, veins, and capillaries. Arteries carry blood away from the heart, while veins carry blood back to the heart. Capillaries are the smallest blood vessels and are responsible for exchanging oxygen, nutrients, and waste products between the blood and the body's tissues.

Blood is a complex fluid that is made up of red blood cells, white blood cells, platelets, and plasma. Red blood cells are responsible for carrying oxygen throughout the body, while white blood cells are responsible for fighting infections. Platelets are responsible for clotting blood when there is an injury, and plasma is the liquid part of the blood that carries nutrients, hormones, and waste products.

The circulatory system is essential for maintaining good health. If any part of the system fails to function properly, it can lead to serious health problems. Some common circulatory system disorders include hypertension, heart disease, and stroke.

In order to maintain a healthy circulatory system, it is important to eat a healthy diet, exercise regularly, and avoid smoking and excessive alcohol consumption. Regular check-ups with a healthcare provider can also help to detect any potential problems early on.

In conclusion, the circulatory system is a vital part of the human body. It plays a crucial role in maintaining good health and must be cared for properly to prevent serious health problems. By understanding how the circulatory system works and taking steps to keep it healthy, we can live longer, healthier lives.

The respiratory system

The respiratory system is an essential part of our body, responsible for the exchange of gases between the body and the environment. It consists of the lungs, bronchi, trachea, and nasal passages.

The lungs are the primary organs of the respiratory system and are responsible for the exchange of gases. The left lung is smaller than the right lung and has two lobes, while the right lung has three lobes. The bronchi are the two tubes that connect the lungs to the trachea. The trachea, also known as the windpipe, is a tube that connects the throat to the lungs. The nasal passages are responsible for filtering and warming the air we breathe.

The respiratory system works in conjunction with the circulatory system to transport oxygen to the body's cells and remove carbon dioxide. Oxygen is taken in through the lungs and transported to the body's cells through the bloodstream. Carbon dioxide is then removed from the body through the lungs.

The respiratory system can be affected by a variety of conditions, including asthma, chronic obstructive pulmonary disease (COPD), pneumonia, and lung cancer. It is essential to maintain good respiratory health through regular exercise, a healthy diet, and avoiding smoking and other environmental pollutants.

When studying for the Hesi A2, it is important to understand the anatomy and physiology of the respiratory system, as well as common respiratory disorders and their treatments. Questions related to the respiratory system may appear on the anatomy and physiology section of the exam, as well as on the science section.

In conclusion, the respiratory system plays a vital role in our body's overall health and well-being. Understanding its anatomy and physiology, as well as common disorders and treatments, is crucial when preparing for the Hesi A2 exam. By taking care of our respiratory health, we can ensure that our body functions properly and efficiently.

The digestive system

The digestive system is a complex network of organs and tissues that work together to break down and absorb nutrients from the food we eat. This system is essential for maintaining the proper functioning of our bodies and keeping us healthy.

The digestive process begins in the mouth, where food is broken down by chewing and mixed with saliva. The food then travels down the esophagus and into the stomach, where it is further broken down by stomach acid and enzymes.

After leaving the stomach, the food enters the small intestine, where the majority of nutrient absorption takes place. The walls of the small intestine are lined with tiny finger-like projections called villi, which increase the surface area available for nutrient absorption.

43

The remaining waste products then enter the large intestine, where water is absorbed and the waste is prepared for elimination from the body.

Several organs play a crucial role in the digestive process, including the liver, pancreas, and gallbladder. The liver produces bile, which helps to break down fats, while the pancreas produces enzymes that aid in the digestion of carbohydrates, proteins, and fats. The gallbladder stores and releases bile as needed.

Maintaining a healthy digestive system is essential for overall health and wellbeing. Eating a balanced diet that is rich in fiber and staying hydrated can help keep the digestive system functioning properly. Regular exercise can also promote healthy digestion.

During the HESI A2 exam, it is important to have a basic understanding of the digestive system and how it works. Questions related to the digestive system may cover topics such as nutrient absorption, the role of specific organs, and common digestive disorders.

By familiarizing themselves with the digestive system and related concepts, test-takers can feel confident and well-prepared for the HESI A2 exam.

The urinary system

The urinary system is a vital part of the human body responsible for removing waste products from the blood and eliminating them from the body through urine. It consists of two kidneys, two ureters, the bladder, and the urethra.

The kidneys play a crucial role in the urinary system as they filter waste products from the blood, regulate electrolyte balance, and produce hormones that control blood pressure and red blood cell production. The ureters transport urine from the kidneys to the bladder, which stores the urine until it is ready to be eliminated from the body through the urethra.

The urinary system is susceptible to several disorders, including urinary tract infections, kidney stones, and bladder cancer. It is essential to maintain good urinary health by drinking plenty of fluids, maintaining good hygiene, and seeking prompt medical attention for any urinary symptoms.

The Hesi A2 exam may test your knowledge of the urinary system, including its anatomy, physiology, and common disorders. You may be asked to identify the different parts of the urinary system or describe how the kidneys function. You may also be asked to recognize the signs and symptoms of urinary tract infections or kidney stones.

To prepare for the urinary system questions on the Hesi A2 exam, it is essential to review the anatomy and physiology of the urinary system thoroughly. You should also familiarize yourself with common urinary disorders and their symptoms. Practice questions and quizzes can help reinforce your understanding of the urinary system and prepare you for the exam.

In summary, the urinary system is a vital part of the human body responsible for removing waste products from the blood and eliminating them from the body through urine. It consists of the kidneys, ureters, bladder, and urethra and is susceptible to several disorders. To prepare for urinary system questions on the Hesi A2 exam, it is essential to review the anatomy and physiology of the urinary system and familiarize yourself with common urinary disorders and their symptoms.

The reproductive system

The reproductive system is an essential part of the human anatomy. It is responsible for the continuity of the human species, and its efficient functioning ensures the perpetuation of life. The reproductive system comprises various organs and structures that work together to produce gametes and facilitate fertilization, pregnancy, and childbirth. In this section, we will discuss the key components of the reproductive system and their functions.

Male Reproductive System:

The male reproductive system comprises the testes, epididymis, vas deferens, prostate gland, seminal vesicles, urethra, and penis. The testes produce sperm, and the epididymis stores and matures them. The vas deferens carries the sperm from the epididymis to the prostate gland, where it mixes with seminal fluid from the seminal vesicles. The mixture of sperm and seminal fluid forms semen, which is ejaculated through the urethra and penis during sexual intercourse.

Female Reproductive System:

The female reproductive system comprises the ovaries, fallopian tubes, uterus, cervix, and vagina. The ovaries produce eggs, which are released into the fallopian tubes during ovulation. The fertilization of the egg by sperm occurs in the fallopian tubes. The fertilized egg then travels to the uterus, where it implants and develops into a fetus. The cervix is the lower part of the uterus that opens into the vagina, which serves as the birth canal during childbirth.

Reproductive Health:

Maintaining reproductive health is crucial for both men and women. Regular check-ups with a healthcare provider can help detect and prevent reproductive system disorders and diseases. Some common reproductive system disorders include infertility, sexually transmitted infections, prostate cancer, ovarian cancer, cervical cancer, and endometriosis. Preventing these conditions involves practicing safe sex, getting vaccinated against sexually transmitted infections, and undergoing regular screenings.

In conclusion, the reproductive system plays a critical role in human reproduction and overall health. Understanding its anatomy and functions is essential for anyone preparing for the Hesi A2 exam. By studying this chapter, aspiring healthcare professionals will gain a thorough understanding of the reproductive system, its health implications, and the importance of maintaining reproductive health.

BIOLOGY

Basic principles of biology

Basic Principles of Biology

Biology is the study of living organisms and their interactions with the environment. It encompasses a wide range of topics, from the smallest cells to entire ecosystems. In order to understand the complexities of biology, it's important to understand some basic principles.

Cell Theory

The cell theory states that all living things are composed of cells. Cells are the basic units of structure and function in living organisms. They can be prokaryotic, which means they lack a nucleus, or eukaryotic, which means they have a nucleus. Cells also have different organelles that perform specific functions within the cell.

Evolution

Evolution is the process by which species change over time. It occurs through natural selection, where organisms with advantageous traits are more likely to survive and reproduce. Over time, these traits become more common in the population, leading to new species.

Homeostasis

Homeostasis is the maintenance of a stable internal environment in living organisms. It involves regulating things like temperature, pH, and nutrient levels. This is important for the survival of organisms, as changes in the environment can be detrimental to their health.

Energy

Living organisms require energy to carry out their various functions. This energy is obtained through the process of respiration, where organisms take in oxygen and release carbon dioxide. Photosynthesis is another important process, where plants use sunlight to produce energy-rich molecules like glucose.

Genetics

Genetics is the study of heredity and how traits are passed down from one generation to the next. It involves the study of DNA, which contains the genetic information that determines an organism's traits.

Conclusion

Understanding these basic principles of biology is essential for success on the Hesi A2 exam. They provide a foundation for more complex topics, and are the building blocks of our understanding of living organisms. By mastering these principles, you'll be better equipped to tackle the more challenging questions on the exam.

Cell structure and function

Cell structure and function are essential topics to understand when preparing for the Hesi A2 exam. Cells are the basic unit of life and are responsible for carrying out all of the functions necessary for an organism to survive. Understanding the structure and function of cells is crucial to understanding the biological processes that occur in the human body.

The cell has several components, including the cell membrane, cytoplasm, and nucleus. The cell membrane is a semi-permeable layer that surrounds the cell, providing a barrier between the cell's internal environment and the external environment. The cytoplasm is the jelly-like substance within the cell that contains organelles, such as mitochondria and ribosomes, which carry out specific functions. The nucleus is the control center of the cell that contains DNA, the genetic material that determines the cell's characteristics.

The function of cells is diverse and complex. Cells carry out processes such as metabolism, growth, and reproduction. Metabolism is the process by which cells convert nutrients into energy. Growth is the process by which cells increase in size and number. Reproduction is the process by which cells divide to create new cells.

Different types of cells have specialized functions. For example, nerve cells are responsible for transmitting signals throughout the body, while muscle cells are responsible for movement. Red blood cells are responsible for carrying oxygen throughout the body, while white blood cells are responsible for fighting infections.

In summary, understanding cell structure and function is crucial for success on the Hesi A2 exam. Cells are the basic unit of life, and their structure and function dictate the biological processes that occur in the human body. Studying cell structure and function will provide a strong foundation for success on the exam and in future healthcare careers.

Genetics and heredity

Genetics and Heredity

Genetics and heredity are key concepts that are tested on the HESI A2 exam. Genetics refers to the study of genes and heredity, while heredity is the passing of traits from one generation to the next. Understanding these concepts is important for nursing students as it can help in identifying and treating genetic disorders.

Genes are the basic units of heredity, and they determine the traits that are passed on from one generation to the next. Each gene is made up of a sequence of nucleotides, which are the building blocks of DNA. The DNA sequence of each gene determines the specific trait that it controls.

Heredity is the process by which traits are passed on from one generation to the next. Traits can be either dominant or recessive. Dominant traits are those that are expressed even if only one copy of the gene is present, while recessive traits are only expressed if two copies of the gene are present.

There are also sex-linked traits, which are controlled by genes located on the X or Y chromosome. In females, there are two X chromosomes, while males have one X and one Y chromosome. This means that males only need one copy of a recessive sex-linked gene to express the trait, while females need two copies.

Genetic disorders are caused by mutations in genes, which can lead to abnormal traits or diseases. Some genetic disorders are inherited in a dominant or recessive manner, while others are caused by mutations in sex-linked genes. Examples of genetic disorders include sickle cell anemia, cystic fibrosis, and Huntington's disease.

In conclusion, genetics and heredity are important concepts for nursing students to understand. A thorough understanding of these concepts can help in identifying and treating genetic disorders. It is important to note that genetic testing and counseling can help individuals and families understand their risk for inherited diseases and make informed decisions regarding their health.

Evolution and natural selection

Evolution and natural selection are important topics to understand when preparing for the HESI A2 exam. These concepts are fundamental to the science of biology and have been studied for centuries by scientists and researchers alike. In this chapter, we will explore the basic principles of evolution and natural selection, and how they apply to the world around us.

Evolution is the process by which species change over time. This change can occur through several mechanisms, including genetic drift, gene flow, and natural selection. Natural selection, in particular, is a powerful force that can shape the characteristics of a species over time.

Natural selection is the process by which organisms with advantageous traits are more likely to survive and reproduce than those without these traits. This leads to the gradual accumulation of beneficial traits within a population, and eventually, the emergence of new species. For example, if a species of bird has a variation in beak size, those with larger beaks may be better able to crack open tough seeds and survive, while those with smaller beaks may struggle to find enough food. Over time, the population may evolve to have larger beaks on average, as those with this trait are more likely to pass it on to their offspring.

It's important to note that natural selection doesn't always lead to the "best" or most advanced traits. Rather, it simply favors those traits that are most beneficial in a particular environment. For example, a species of fish living in a dark cave may evolve to have no eyes, as this trait is not useful in this environment.

Overall, understanding evolution and natural selection is key to success on the HESI A2 exam. These concepts are essential to understanding the diversity of life on Earth and the processes that have shaped it over time. By studying these topics, you will gain a deeper appreciation for the complexity and beauty of the natural world.

Ecology and environmental science

Ecology and environmental science are two of the most important topics that are covered in the Hesi A2 exam. These subjects delve into the relationship between organisms and their environment, and how these interactions impact the natural world.

Ecology is the study of how living organisms interact with each other and their environment. It encompasses the study of populations, communities, and ecosystems. In essence, it is the study of the relationships between living organisms and their physical surroundings. Environmental science, on the other hand, is the study of the impact of human activity on the natural world. It encompasses the study of environmental pollution, resource depletion, and climate change.

Both ecology and environmental science are critical to our understanding of the natural world and how we can protect it. It is important to note that human activities have a profound effect on the environment. For example, pollution from factories and vehicles can contaminate water and air, while deforestation can lead to soil erosion and loss of biodiversity.

To address these issues, it is essential to have a comprehensive understanding of ecology and environmental science. This includes understanding the natural processes that occur in the environment, as well as the impact of human activities on these processes.

The Hesi A2 exam will test your knowledge of these subjects, and it is crucial to prepare accordingly. Some of the topics that you should be familiar with include the carbon cycle, water cycle, food webs, and energy transfer in ecosystems. You should also be familiar with environmental laws and regulations, such as the Clean Air Act and Clean Water Act.

In conclusion, ecology and environmental science are vital topics that are covered in the Hesi A2 exam. By understanding these subjects, we can better understand the impact of human activities on the natural world and take steps to protect it. To prepare for the exam, it is essential to have a solid understanding of these topics and their applications in the real world.

CHEMISTRY

Basic principles of chemistry

Basic Principles of Chemistry

Chemistry is the science that studies the composition, properties, and behavior of matter. In order to understand the principles of chemistry, it is important to have a basic knowledge of the structure of matter.

Atoms are the basic building blocks of matter. They are made up of protons, neutrons, and electrons. Protons have a positive charge, neutrons have no charge, and electrons have a negative charge. The number of protons determines the element to which the atom belongs, and the number of electrons determines the atom's charge. Atoms can form compounds by sharing or transferring electrons.

One of the most important concepts in chemistry is the periodic table. The periodic table is a chart that organizes the elements by their atomic number, electron configuration, and chemical properties. It is a useful tool for predicting the behavior of elements and their compounds.

Chemical reactions involve the breaking and forming of chemical bonds. The reactants are the starting materials, and the products are the substances that are formed as a result of the reaction. Chemical reactions can be classified as exothermic or endothermic, depending on whether energy is released or absorbed during the reaction.

Acids and bases are important concepts in chemistry. Acids are substances that donate hydrogen ions (H+) in water, while bases are substances that accept hydrogen ions or donate hydroxide ions (OH-) in water. The pH scale is used to measure the acidity or basicity of a solution, with a pH of 7 being neutral, a pH less than 7 being acidic, and a pH greater than 7 being basic.

Organic chemistry is the study of carbon-based compounds, which are essential to life. Carbon can form four covalent bonds, allowing it to form a wide variety of compounds. Organic compounds include carbohydrates, lipids, proteins, and nucleic acids.

In conclusion, understanding the basic principles of chemistry is essential for success in the Hesi A2 exam. From the structure of atoms to the behavior of compounds, chemistry is a fascinating and important science that plays a crucial role in our daily lives.

Atomic structure and bonding

Atomic structure and bonding are fundamental concepts in chemistry, and they play a critical role in understanding the physical and chemical properties of matter. The Hesi A2 exam assesses the knowledge of these concepts among the students who wish to pursue a career in the field of healthcare.

The atom is the basic unit of matter, and it consists of three subatomic particles: protons, neutrons, and electrons. Protons are positively charged particles found in the nucleus of an atom, while neutrons are neutral particles also located in the nucleus. Electrons are negatively charged particles that orbit the nucleus in shells or energy levels.

The number of protons in the nucleus of an atom determines its atomic number and its identity as an element. For example, an atom with one proton is hydrogen, while an atom with six protons is carbon. The number of neutrons in an atom's nucleus can vary, resulting in different isotopes of the same element.

The electrons in an atom's outermost shell determine its chemical properties and reactivity. Atoms with a full outer shell of electrons are stable and unreactive, while those with an incomplete outer shell are reactive and tend to form chemical bonds with other atoms.

Chemical bonding occurs when atoms share or transfer electrons to form a stable compound. There are three types of chemical bonds: covalent, ionic, and metallic. In covalent bonding, atoms share electrons to fill their outer shells, forming a molecule. In ionic bonding, one atom donates an electron to another, resulting in positively and negatively charged ions that attract each other. In metallic bonding, electrons are shared among a group of atoms, creating a lattice structure.

Understanding atomic structure and bonding is essential for various fields of healthcare, including pharmacology, biochemistry, and microbiology. For example, the structure of a drug molecule determines its interactions with the body and its effectiveness in treating a particular disease.

In conclusion, atomic structure and bonding are fundamental concepts that play a critical role in understanding the physical and chemical properties of matter. A thorough understanding of these concepts is essential for success in various fields of healthcare, and it is crucial to prepare well for the Hesi A2 exam.

Chemical reactions and equations

Chemical reactions and equations are an essential part of the Hesi A2 exam and understanding the basic concepts is crucial. Chemical reactions are the process by which two or more substances interact to form a new substance. These reactions can be classified into different types based on the nature of the reactants and products.

One of the most common types of chemical reactions is the combination reaction. In this type of reaction, two or more substances combine to form a new product. For example, the reaction between hydrogen and oxygen to form water is a combination reaction.

Another type of reaction is the decomposition reaction. In this type of reaction, a single compound breaks down into two or more simpler substances. The reaction between hydrogen peroxide and water to form oxygen and water is a decomposition reaction.

A single displacement reaction is a reaction in which an element or ion in a compound is replaced by another element or ion. For example, the reaction between zinc and hydrochloric acid to form zinc chloride and hydrogen gas is a single displacement reaction.

A double displacement reaction is a reaction in which two compounds exchange ions or atoms to form two new compounds. For example, the reaction between sodium chloride and silver nitrate to form silver chloride and sodium nitrate is a double displacement reaction.

Chemical equations are used to represent chemical reactions. In a chemical equation, the reactants are written on the left-hand side of the equation, and the products are written on the right-hand side. The equation must be balanced, which means that the number of atoms of each element must be the same on both sides of the equation.

In conclusion, understanding the basic concepts of chemical reactions and equations is essential for the Hesi A2 exam. It is important to be familiar with the different types of reactions and how to balance chemical equations. With practice and study, you can master this topic and ace the Hesi A2 exam.

Acids and bases

Acids and bases are two essential components of chemistry that are commonly tested in the Hesi A2 exam. Understanding the properties of these substances is crucial to success in the chemistry section of the exam. In this subchapter, we will explore what acids and bases are, their properties, and their applications.

Acids are defined as substances that donate hydrogen ions (H+) in a chemical reaction. They have a pH value of less than 7 and can be identified by their sour taste and ability to dissolve metals. Examples of common acids include hydrochloric acid, nitric acid, and sulfuric acid.

Bases, on the other hand, are substances that accept hydrogen ions (H+) in a chemical reaction. They have a pH value of more than 7 and are characterized by their bitter taste and slippery texture. Examples of common bases include sodium hydroxide, potassium hydroxide, and ammonia.

One of the most important properties of acids and bases is their ability to neutralize each other. When an acid and a base are mixed, they react to form a salt and water. This reaction is called neutralization and is used in various applications like antacids, which neutralize stomach acid, and the production of soap.

Another essential property of acids and bases is their strength. Strong acids and bases completely dissociate in water to form ions, while weak acids and bases only partially dissociate. The strength of an acid or base is measured using the pH scale, which ranges from 0 to 14, with 7 being neutral. The lower the pH value, the stronger the acid, and the higher the pH value, the stronger the base.

In conclusion, understanding the properties of acids and bases is crucial to success in the chemistry section of the Hesi A2 exam. Acids and bases have different properties and applications, and their strength is measured using the pH scale. By mastering these concepts, you will be well-prepared to tackle any acid-base related questions in the exam.

Organic chemistry

Organic chemistry is a branch of chemistry that deals with the study of carbon-containing compounds, which are the building blocks of life. This subchapter will cover the basic concepts of organic chemistry that you need to know for the Hesi A2 exam.

Firstly, it is important to understand the nature of carbon. Carbon has four valence electrons, which means it can form up to four covalent bonds with other atoms, such as hydrogen, oxygen, nitrogen, and sulfur. These covalent bonds are strong and stable, which makes carbon compounds versatile and complex.

One of the most important concepts in organic chemistry is functional groups. These are specific groups of atoms that give a molecule its characteristic properties and reactivity. For example, the hydroxyl group (-OH) is found in alcohols, which are characterized by their ability to dissolve in water and participate in hydrogen bonding. The carboxyl group (-COOH) is found in organic acids, which are characterized by their acidic properties and ability to donate hydrogen ions.

Another important concept in organic chemistry is isomerism. Isomers are molecules that have the same molecular formula but different structures. For example, glucose and fructose are isomers of each other, even though they have the same chemical formula ($C_6H_{12}O_6$). Isomerism is important because it can affect the physical and chemical properties of a molecule, such as its melting point, boiling point, and reactivity.

The Hesi A2 exam may also test your knowledge of organic reactions, such as substitution, addition, and elimination. These reactions involve the breaking and forming of covalent bonds, which can result in the formation of new molecules with different properties. For example, the reaction between an alkene and hydrogen gas (H2) can result in the formation of an alkane, which is a saturated hydrocarbon.

In summary, organic chemistry is a complex and fascinating field that involves the study of carbon-containing compounds and their properties. Understanding the basic concepts of organic chemistry, such as functional groups, isomerism, and organic reactions, can help you ace the Hesi A2 exam and succeed in your future healthcare career.

PHYSICS

Basic principles of physics

Basic Principles of Physics

Physics is the branch of science that deals with the study of matter, energy, and their interactions. It is a fundamental part of the Hesi A2 exam, and understanding the basic principles of physics is crucial for success in this exam. The principles of physics are used in many fields, including medicine, engineering, and technology. In this subchapter, we will discuss some of the basic principles of physics that you need to know for the Hesi A2 exam.

The first basic principle of physics is the law of conservation of energy. This law states that energy cannot be created or destroyed, only converted from one form to another. This means that the total amount of energy in a closed system remains constant. For example, when a ball is thrown, the potential energy is converted into kinetic energy, and the total energy of the ball remains constant.

The second basic principle of physics is Newton's laws of motion. These laws describe the relationship between the motion of an object and the forces acting on it. The first law states that an object at rest will remain at rest, and an object in motion will remain in motion unless acted upon by an external force. The second law states that the acceleration of an object is directly proportional to the force applied to it and inversely proportional to its mass. The third law states that for every action, there is an equal and opposite reaction.

Another important principle of physics is the concept of work and power. Work is defined as the product of force and distance, while power is the rate at which work is done. Understanding these concepts is important for understanding the efficiency of machines and the amount of energy required to perform a task.

Finally, the principle of heat transfer is also important for the Hesi A2 exam. Heat transfer occurs when there is a temperature difference between two objects, and it can occur through conduction, convection, and radiation.

Knowledge of these principles is important for understanding how heat is transferred in the human body and in various medical procedures.

In conclusion, understanding the basic principles of physics is crucial for success in the Hesi A2 exam. These principles are used in many fields, and a strong foundation in physics will be useful throughout your academic and professional career.

Motion and forces

Motion and forces are essential concepts in physics that are often tested in the Hesi A2 exam. Understanding these concepts is crucial for success in the exam and in many science-related fields. In this subchapter, we will discuss the key concepts related to motion and forces that you need to know for the Hesi A2 exam.

Motion refers to the change in position of an object relative to a frame of reference. It can be described using different terms such as speed, velocity, and acceleration. Speed is the rate at which an object moves, while velocity is the speed of an object in a particular direction. Acceleration is the rate at which the velocity of an object changes. These concepts are often tested in the Hesi A2 exam, so it's important to understand the differences between them.

Forces are interactions between two objects that cause a change in motion. There are four fundamental forces in nature: gravitational, electromagnetic, strong, and weak. However, for the Hesi A2 exam, you only need to understand the basic concepts of force, such as Newton's laws of motion. Newton's first law states that an object at rest will remain at rest, and an object in motion will remain in motion at a constant velocity unless acted upon by a net force. Newton's second law states that the acceleration of an object is directly proportional to the net force applied to it and inversely proportional to its mass. Newton's third law states that for every action, there is an equal and opposite reaction.

In conclusion, motion and forces are important concepts that are tested in the Hesi A2 exam. Understanding the differences between concepts such as speed, velocity, and acceleration, as well as the basic laws of motion, is crucial for success in the exam. Make sure to review these concepts thoroughly before taking the exam to ensure your success.

Energy and work

Energy and work are two concepts that are closely related and often used interchangeably. In physics, energy refers to the ability of an object to do work. Work, on the other hand, is the transfer of energy from one object to another. Understanding the relationship between energy and work is crucial for success in the Hesi A2 exam.

Energy can take many forms, including mechanical, thermal, electrical, and chemical. These different types of energy are all related and can be converted from one form to another. For example, the chemical energy stored in food can be converted to mechanical energy to power our muscles. Similarly, electrical energy can be converted to light energy in a light bulb.

Work, on the other hand, is defined as the force applied to an object over a distance. This means that work is done when an object is moved against a force. For example, lifting a heavy object requires work to be done against the force of gravity.

In order to calculate the amount of work done, we need to know both the force applied and the distance over which it was applied. The formula for work is $W = Fd$, where W is work, F is force, and d is distance. The unit of work is the joule (J), which is defined as the amount of work done when a force of one newton is applied over a distance of one meter.

Energy and work are related through the concept of conservation of energy. This law states that energy cannot be created or destroyed, only transferred from one object to another. Therefore, the amount of work done on an object is equal to the change in its energy. This means that when work is done on an object, its energy increases, and when work is done by an object, its energy decreases.

In summary, energy and work are two fundamental concepts in physics that are closely related. Understanding the relationship between these concepts is crucial for success in the Hesi A2 exam. Remember that energy cannot be created or destroyed, only transferred from one object to another, and that work is the transfer of energy from one object to another.

Waves and sound

Waves and Sound

Understanding the principles of waves and sound is an important aspect of the Hesi A2 exam. Waves are a common phenomenon that we observe in our daily lives. From the movement of ocean waves to the sound waves that we hear, waves are present all around us.

A wave is defined as a disturbance that travels through a medium, transferring energy from one point to another without any transfer of matter. Waves can be classified into two types: mechanical waves and electromagnetic waves.

Mechanical waves require a medium to travel through, such as a solid, liquid, or gas. These waves include sound waves, water waves, and seismic waves. The speed of mechanical waves is dependent on the properties of the medium they travel through.

Electromagnetic waves, on the other hand, do not require a medium to travel through. These waves include visible light, radio waves, microwaves, x-rays, and gamma rays. The speed of electromagnetic waves is constant and is equal to the speed of light.

Sound waves are a type of mechanical wave that travels through a medium, such as air or water. They are produced by a vibrating object, which causes the particles in the medium to vibrate. These vibrations then travel through the medium as a wave, which we perceive as sound.

The properties of sound waves include frequency, wavelength, and amplitude. Frequency is the number of vibrations per second and is measured in hertz (Hz). Wavelength is the distance between two consecutive points in a wave and is measured in meters (m). Amplitude is the maximum displacement of the medium from its rest position and is measured in decibels (dB).

Understanding waves and sound is essential for a variety of fields, including physics, medicine, and engineering. The Hesi A2 exam may test your knowledge of these concepts, so be sure to review them thoroughly before taking the exam.

Light and optics

Light and optics are important concepts that are covered on the Hesi A2 exam. These concepts are essential for understanding how light travels and how our eyes perceive light. In this subchapter, we will explore the basics of light and optics, including the properties of light, reflection, refraction, and lenses.

Light is a form of energy that travels in waves. The properties of light include its wavelength, frequency, and amplitude. The wavelength of light determines its color, with longer wavelengths appearing red and shorter wavelengths appearing blue. The frequency of light determines its energy, with higher frequencies having more energy. The amplitude of light determines its brightness, with higher amplitudes appearing brighter.

Reflection is the process by which light bounces off a surface. The angle of incidence, or the angle at which the light hits the surface, is equal to the angle of reflection, or the angle at which the light bounces off the surface. This is why we can see our reflection in a mirror.

Refraction is the process by which light changes direction as it passes through a medium with a different density. This is why a straw appears to bend when it is placed in a glass of water. The amount of refraction depends on the angle of incidence and the difference in density between the two media.

Lenses are curved pieces of glass or plastic that can refract light. There are two types of lenses: convex and concave. A convex lens is thicker in the middle and thinner at the edges, and it can focus light to create a sharp image. A concave lens is thinner in the middle and thicker at the edges, and it spreads out light to create a blurry image.

Understanding the basics of light and optics is essential for many fields, including physics, astronomy, and optometry. By mastering these concepts, you will be better equipped to answer questions on the Hesi A2 exam and succeed in your academic and professional endeavors.

FINAL TIPS AND RESOURCES FOR THE HESI A2 EXAM

Final words of advice

As you approach the completion of your Hesi A2 exam preparation, it is essential to remember a few crucial pieces of advice. These final words of advice will help you maintain confidence, focus, and motivation as you prepare for the exam and take it on the day.

Firstly, it is critical to focus on your strengths rather than your weaknesses. While it is essential to identify and address your weaknesses, it is equally important to celebrate your strengths, as this will boost your confidence and motivation. Be proud of your strengths and use them to your advantage during the exam.

Secondly, create a study plan that is customized to your learning style and schedule. A study plan will help you stay on track, manage your time effectively, and ensure that you cover all the topics you need to know. Make sure to allocate enough time for each topic, and don't forget to take breaks to avoid burnout.

Thirdly, practice, practice, practice. Practice exams, quizzes, and flashcards are excellent tools to help you prepare for the Hesi A2 exam. Practice exams will help you identify your weaknesses, and quizzes and flashcards will help you reinforce your knowledge.

Fourthly, take care of yourself. A healthy body and mind are essential for exam success. Make sure to get enough sleep, eat well, exercise, and take breaks when needed. Taking care of yourself will help you stay focused, motivated, and reduce stress levels.

Lastly, on the day of the exam, remember to stay calm and focused. Take deep breaths, read the questions carefully, and don't rush. Remember that you have prepared for this exam, and you are ready.

In conclusion, the Hesi A2 exam can be challenging, but with the right preparation, mindset, and attitude, you can ace it. Remember to focus on your strengths, create a customized study plan, practice, take care of yourself, and stay calm on the day of the exam. Good luck!

Additional resources for study

Additional resources for study

Preparing for the HESI A2 can be a daunting task, but it doesn't have to be. There are many resources available to help you ace the exam and achieve your academic goals.

Here are some additional resources you can use to supplement your study efforts.

1. Online practice tests

There are many online practice tests available that simulate the HESI A2 exam. These tests can help you get a feel for the types of questions you'll see on the actual exam and help you identify areas where you need more practice. Some popular sites for HESI A2 practice tests include TestPrep-Online, HESI Exam Guide, and Mometrix.

2. Study guides

Many publishers offer study guides specifically tailored to the HESI A2 exam. These guides typically cover all the topics that will be tested on the exam and provide test-taking strategies and tips. Some popular HESI A2 study guides include the HESI A2 Secrets Study Guide by Mometrix and the HESI A2 Study Guide 2023-2024 by Test Prep Books.

3. Flashcards

Flashcards are a great tool for memorizing key concepts and terms. There are many HESI A2 flashcard sets available online or in bookstores. Some popular options include the HESI A2 Flashcard Study System by Mometrix and the HESI A2 Flashcards 2023-2024 by Test Prep Books.

4. Tutoring services

If you're struggling with a particular subject or concept, consider hiring a tutor. Many tutoring services offer HESI A2-specific tutoring, either in-person or online. Tutoring can be particularly helpful if you're struggling with math or science, which are often the most challenging sections of the exam.

5. Study groups

Joining or forming a study group can be a great way to stay motivated and learn from your peers. Study groups can be particularly helpful if you're struggling with a particular topic or need help with test-taking strategies. Many schools and universities offer HESI A2 study groups, or you can start your own with classmates or friends.

In conclusion, while preparing for the HESI A2 exam can be challenging, there are many resources available to help you succeed. Utilizing online practice tests, study guides, flashcards, tutoring services, and study groups can all help you improve your test-taking skills and achieve your academic goals. Good luck!

Frequently asked questions about the Hesi A2

Frequently asked questions about the Hesi A2

As you prepare for the Hesi A2 exam, you may have a lot of questions about what to expect and how to best prepare. Here are some frequently asked questions about the Hesi A2, along with answers to help you prepare for success.

Q: What is the Hesi A2 exam?
A: The Hesi A2 (Health Education Systems, Inc. Admission Assessment) exam is a standardized test used by many nursing schools and other healthcare programs to evaluate applicants. It covers topics such as math, reading comprehension, vocabulary, grammar, anatomy and physiology, and more.

Q: How long is the Hesi A2 exam?
A: The Hesi A2 exam can vary in length, depending on the specific program you are applying to. It typically takes around 4 hours to complete all sections of the exam.

Q: What is a passing score for the Hesi A2 exam?
A: Passing scores for the Hesi A2 exam vary by program. Some programs may require a minimum score of 75% or higher, while others may require a minimum score of 80% or higher. It's important to check with the specific program you are applying to for their requirements.

Q: What topics are covered on the Hesi A2 exam?
A: The Hesi A2 exam covers a wide range of topics, including math, reading comprehension, vocabulary, grammar, anatomy and physiology, and more. It's important to review all of these topics thoroughly in order to perform well on the exam.

Q: How can I best prepare for the Hesi A2 exam?
A: There are many ways to prepare for the Hesi A2 exam, including studying with a Hesi A2 study guide, taking practice exams, reviewing course materials, and working with a tutor or study group. It's important to find the method that works best for you and to dedicate enough time to prepare thoroughly.

Q: Can I retake the Hesi A2 exam if I don't pass?
A: Yes, most programs allow you to retake the Hesi A2 exam if you don't pass on your first attempt. However, there may be limitations on how many times you can retake the exam or how long you have to wait between attempts.

By understanding what to expect on the Hesi A2 exam and how to best prepare, you can increase your chances of success and achieve your goals of entering a nursing or healthcare program.

CONCLUSION

Summary of key points

The Hesi A2 exam is a crucial step for anyone aspiring to pursue a career in healthcare. However, studying for this exam can be overwhelming, especially if you are unsure of the format and content of the questions. This is where the "Ace the Hesi A2: Your Ultimate Study Guide for 2023-2024" comes in. This book is a comprehensive guide that covers all the topics included in the Hesi A2 exam, making it the perfect tool to help you prepare for this important test.

In this subchapter, we summarize the key points covered in this guide. Firstly, we highlight the importance of understanding the structure of the Hesi A2 exam. The exam consists of several sections, including math, reading comprehension, vocabulary, grammar, anatomy and physiology, and chemistry. It is essential to know the format of each section, the number of questions, and the time allotted for each section.

Secondly, we emphasize the significance of practicing with Hesi A2 sample questions. This book provides numerous sample questions, which are similar to those asked in the actual exam. Solving these questions will help you become familiar with the exam format, improve your time management skills, and identify areas where you need to focus your study efforts.

Thirdly, we stress the importance of understanding the concepts covered in the exam. This guide covers all the topics included in the Hesi A2 exam, including math formulas, anatomy and physiology concepts, and chemistry principles. Understanding these topics is crucial for solving the exam questions correctly.

Lastly, we highlight the importance of time management during the exam. The Hesi A2 exam is time-limited, and you need to be able to manage your time effectively to answer all the questions before the time runs out. This guide provides tips and strategies for time management during the exam, ensuring that you can complete the exam within the given time frame.

In conclusion, the "Ace the Hesi A2: Your Ultimate Study Guide for 2023-2024" is an essential tool for anyone preparing for the Hesi A2 exam. It provides comprehensive coverage of all the topics included in the exam, sample questions for practice, and time management strategies. By following the tips and strategies outlined in this guide, you can ace the Hesi A2 exam and take a step closer to your dream career in healthcare.

Importance of preparation for the Hesi A2

Preparing for the Hesi A2 exam is crucial to achieving a high score and gaining admission to your desired nursing program. The Hesi A2 exam is a comprehensive test that assesses your knowledge and skills in various areas such as math, science, reading comprehension, and critical thinking. In this subchapter, we will discuss the importance of preparation for the Hesi A2 exam.

Firstly, preparation is essential to familiarize yourself with the exam format, types of questions, and time constraints. The Hesi A2 exam is a computer-based test, and being comfortable with the format can help alleviate any anxiety or stress during the actual exam. Knowing the types of questions that will be asked can also help you focus your study efforts on the areas you need to improve.

Secondly, preparation allows you to identify your strengths and weaknesses in different subject areas. By taking practice tests and reviewing your results, you can pinpoint the areas where you need to focus your study efforts. This can help you save time and energy by avoiding spending too much time on subjects you are already proficient in.

Thirdly, preparation can help you build confidence and reduce test anxiety. By studying regularly and taking practice tests, you can increase your confidence in your abilities and reduce stress on the day of the exam. This can help you perform better and achieve a higher score.

Finally, preparation can help you maximize your study time and improve your overall performance. By using study guides and resources specifically designed for the Hesi A2 exam, you can ensure that you are studying the right material and using the most effective study methods. This can help you achieve a higher score and increase your chances of gaining admission to your desired nursing program.

In conclusion, preparation is essential for success on the Hesi A2 exam. By familiarizing yourself with the exam format, identifying your strengths and weaknesses, building confidence, and using effective study methods, you can achieve a high score and gain admission to your dream nursing program.